Turtles

Everything About
Purchase, Care,
and Nutrition

Hartmut Wilke

BARRON'S

Contents

About Turtles

People who want to take care of a turtle can build on forty years of scientific insights. We know the creatures' living conditions in the wild, the composition of their food, and the rhythm of their activity, plus their requirements for living conditions when they are in the care of humans.

The Basics of Living Conditions

With this manual, you have a solid compendium for understanding the basics of owning a turtle. You can use it for planning and becoming familiar with species that are appropriate even for those who are inexperienced at caring for turtles, for it is quite easy to meet these remarkable creatures' living requirements.

Getting Good Information   There is no better preparation than making connections with turtle study groups and associations (see Organizations, page 62). These generally offer a good platform for further training and information exchange.

Getting a Healthy Animal

The basic requirement for enjoying a turtle is to buy a healthy animal. Even newcomers to turtle ownership can tell the difference between healthy and sick animals with the help of the checklist on page 53. Also read my recommendations in this handbook about the best places and times for buying your pet. All this important information starts on page 24.

Quarantine   If you obtain a European tortoise, you will need to consider it a quarantine animal; that is, during this time, you must not put it in with any other animals from different sources. The reason for this is the outbreak of a deadly virus (the Ranavirus), which has been known since the end of 2007 and can present itself after months. It leads to inflammations in the mouth and the eyelids. Since the infection generally occurs in new arrivals, turtle owners have, in the meantime, become very cautious about entering into breeding arrangements with unknown animals.

The Developmental History of Turtles

Today, there are more than 200 species of turtles living on earth. But why are there so many? That is easily explained! Imagine a single, original turtle species that may have existed more than 230 million years ago. Its descendents today would have to be able to survive in the desert and in the oceans, in both hot and cold temperatures, and in the snow. But that simply is not possible.

Splitting into Numerous Species

Turtles were able to pull off this feat only with the help of a magic biological formula, namely, splitting into species through adaptation. Depending on their genetic makeup, turtles moved into different habitats that they could best tolerate and that were not yet inhabited by other species. There, they adapted to the prevailing environmental conditions through such means as changes in their body shape.

Tortoises were thus able to become large and heavy, as long as they had no enemies. On the Galapagos Islands and the Seychelles they grew into real giants.

Aquatic turtles, on the other hand, developed a flat, more streamlined physique. This is a great advantage for them, allowing them to move quickly and efficiently under water.

Different Shell Shapes

Depending on the species, the turtle shell has changed not only its shape but also its structure and solidity. A couple of examples illustrate this:
> With soft-shelled turtles, the shell has regressed to a tough, elastic skin. The defense strategy of this creature involves digging into the sand and making themselves invisible. In addition, they have a very powerful bite when they need to defend themselves.

Turtles are a "recipe for success" through evolution. They have lived on earth for more than 230 million years.

On the Seychelles and the Galapagos Islands, heavy, defenseless tortoises with strongly arched shells were able to develop undisturbed . . .

whereas the West African Mud Turtle, for example, with a flat shell, is well adapted to tropical waters and even to periodic drying up.

> The Pancake Tortoise (*Malacohersus tornieri*) lives on land. It has a very flat shell that has thinned to such an extent that it has become elastic. For protection from enemies, this species withdraws into small cracks in the rocks in its habitat, the African savannah.

> With Eastern Box Turtles (*Terrapene carolina carolina*), the shells have hinges. These make it possible to close up the shell completely once the creature pulls in its head and legs.

Different Ways of Life

Thanks to their great adaptability, turtles, along with crocodiles, have been among the most successful survivors for many millions of years. One important factor in their survival is their ability to adapt to the climatic conditions of their habitat.

Estivation (summer rest) As a reaction to hot, dry desert climates and the sudden onset of the winter cold, the Russian Tortoise (*Testudo horsefieldii*) may only be active for three months of the year. It remains in a deep sleep the rest of the year. In contrast, the aquatic West African Mud Turtle (*Pelusios castaneus*) makes it through the drying up of its home waters by digging into the damp mud. This, likewise, dries out, and only when the ground softens from rain can the turtle become active again.

Hibernation In northern latitudes, turtles generally make it through the cold season by going into a dormant phase. During their active phase, their habitat provides them with all the environmental conditions—adequate sunlight, warm ambient temperatures, and food—in which the individual species have become specialized.

Laying Eggs on Land A basic requirement for every species, whether a sea turtle in the ocean or a soft-shelled turtle on the bottom of a body of water, is that it must be able to get onto solid land to lay eggs.

A Wild Animal Under Human Care

Turtles have developed the ability to adapt over the course of millions of years, but that does not mean they can adapt to poor living conditions in human care. On the contrary, humans need to know their requirements precisely and come as close as possible to those conditions in the terrarium and the outdoor pen. With good care, they can turn into lifelong companions—aquatic turtles live for forty to sixty years, and tortoises can even live to be 100 to 120 years old.

Non-allergenic Turtles can also be a likeable partner for all types of people who are allergic to animal hair or feathers, for they are essentially non-allergenic. They seldom transmit diseases to people.

Cold-blooded Animals

One very important aspect in the life of turtles is that they are cold-blooded. This means they do not control their body temperature themselves, but

Pond turtles, such as this American Box Turtle, are happy when they can hunt their own live food in the outdoor pen. They easily find snails, bugs, isopods, and worms that you put out for them.

rather take it on from their surroundings. Therefore, sunlight is just as important for them as the opportunity to cool off when the temperature gets too high. The animals spend a large part of their day purposefully oscillating between sources of heat and cooling and maintaining their preferred body temperature. This is required not only for proper digestion but also for enabling the immune system and activating metabolism. Failure to meet this requirement in their living conditions is the most common cause of illness and death among turtles.

The Body Language of Turtles

In order to take care of a turtle, you must learn its body language, especially the signs that indicate that it wants to go into hibernation (see page 56). Some aquatic turtles, particularly those in fairly large outdoor pens, react with distinct flight behavior, even when a familiar person appears. This is part of their natural instinct, for when danger looms, they simply drop from their sunning place into the water. This behavior displays their character as wild animals, and you must respect it. But generally, turtles quickly learn to trust the person who takes care of them.

Understanding Behavior Patterns

TIPS FROM
TURTLE EXPERT
Dr. Hartmut Wilke

OBSERVE CLOSELY Become familiar with your turtle and its behavior. Even when it is doing seemingly "nothing," this still means something.

LOOK FOR THE MEANING What is going on with your turtle? Why is it demonstrating a particular behavior such as resting or digging?

SEARCH FOR ANSWERS Find a definitive answer to your question. Of course you may not find it so quickly at the start of your learning process. But you will after a year or so, as long as you keep looking for the meaning of the behavior.

RECOGNIZING BEHAVIORS Without expertise, you run the risk of merely guessing as you interpret the behavior. So take advantage of the descriptions of conspicuous behaviors on page 54, as well as the extensive descriptions in the additional literature (see page 62). In addition, you can ask experienced owners to explain what particular behaviors mean. Consider joining an online chat group to gain answers and insights.

The Basis of Species Protection

Turtle populations in the wild are on the decline worldwide. In order to protect them—and flora and fauna in general—laws are being enacted to regulate the ownership and keeping of animals, as well as their breeding and transfer (regardless of whether as a gift or in exchange for money).

Checking Protection Status You can find out if your pet falls under special protection by inquiring with authorities, such as the appropriate fish and game department, or by checking online (see

Appropriate accommodations are required for ownership authorization issued by appropriate authorities.

Organizations, page 62). I recommend that you get the current information before you buy a turtle; that way you can comply with legal requirements on keeping a turtle. Species with a status of "strictly protected" are generally excluded from being kept as pets.

At Point of Purchase If you are considering purchasing an imported turtle, be sure it comes with the appropriate paperwork. Imported turtles are accompanied by a CITES certificate. All papers should include a "passport photo" by way of photo documentation. Breeders and dealers issue these documents according to regulations and will explain any steps required for legal ownership of the animal.

Turtles are some of the oldest creatures around, having been on the earth for about 250 million years.

A Word About **Wild Turtles**

Taking a turtle from its native habitat to keep as a pet is generally not recommended. It is one thing to observe the "24-hour rule," that is, to bring a wild turtle into your home and keep it for a period of one day or less. You might do this so that your child can have the opportunity to observe a wild turtle close up and develop a better understanding of these remarkable creatures. If you decide to do this, be sure to return the turtle to the place where it was found. Or, if the place it was found is not a safe place (such as the middle of a busy street), return it nearby and heading in the direction that it was moving at the time you found it.

Instead of removing a wild animal from its habitat (which may be illegal in the case of some turtles) always purchase a pet turtle from a reputable dealer. A reputable dealer will provide you with care instructions and detailed information about your new pet, including species, birth date, information about the parent turtles, and any references to an existing breeding record.

Turtles and Children

With careful instruction you can introduce turtle care to your children when they are as young as six. Children generally are very patient, precise observers. They quickly learn to notice changes in behavior—one basic requirement for dealing responsibly with a turtle. Of course you must "train" your child to take care of a turtle. Try it out for yourself before you buy a turtle for a child. You could easily be the one who ends up responsible for the care—for the turtle's lifetime. Your child should understand from the beginning that a turtle is not a cuddly pet. Turtles don't like being picked up constantly. Crawling around on the floor with no place to hide also amounts to little more than a frightening and painful experience.

Turtles and Other Animals

They really are not made for each other, but if you observe the basic precaution "only under my supervision," a meeting generally is permissible—from the turtle's viewpoint.

Dogs and Cats like to sniff curiously at a turtle, tip it over with a paw, or even bite it. From the turtle's viewpoint, this amounts to a threatening encounter. A dog or cat might also appear unconcerned until you leave the room, only making its move on the new "toy" without your supervision. So always keep a sharp eye on your pets.

Rats may be interested in young turtles; however, guinea pigs, hamsters, mice, and song birds should pose no danger.

Outdoors in the pen some animals could be a threat to the turtle. Crows, for example, may peck the eyes out of larger turtles, and like magpies, they may carry off smaller ones as prey. Therefore, turtles kept outdoors need protection (see page 41) during the day and a predator-proof shelter for the night.

The right way: Your pet must not regard the turtle as a toy and must encounter it only in your presence.

Distinguishing Between Tortoises and Aquatic Turtles

For beginners, it is often difficult to tell what a turtle's habitat is just from looking at the turtle. In this manual, I present species from the tortoise, side-necked, European pond, and mud turtle families.

Turtle Identification

Normally, you would expect to purchase a turtle from a reputable dealer who provides information on the turtle's species and care requirements. But, what do you do if a turtle comes into your care without identification? How do you go about identifying such a turtle? The best way to find out what kind of species you have is to seek identification from a reptile expert. You might find such an individual through a zoo or natural history museum in your region. There are many useful turtle websites, but the best identification comes from an expert in the field. It is important to know the species of turtle you are caring for because different animals have different care requirements.

The nose area is blunt and equipped with temperature sensor cells.

The nostrils on the pointed muzzle serve aquatic turtles (bottom) as a "snorkel."

Requirements of the Species Mentioned in This Manual

TRAIT	TORTOISES	AQUATIC TURTLES	SPECIAL CASES BOX TURTLES
SPECIFICATIONS	Large main area needed; water only in a bowl	Mainly water; good swimmers need deep water; poor swimmers need climbing aids	Larger land portion; the water portion takes up about a fifth of the area
KEEP SOLELY IN TERRARIUM	No	Possible depending on species (see page 22ff)	No
TEMPERATURE REQUIREMENTS	See specific temperature requirements for each species in species section	Water must be generally 75–82°F (24–29°C); Need basking, haul-out area with a 50- to 150-watt bulb to create hot spot	Provide warm spot on one side of the enclosure that is 80–85°F (27–29°C). Maintain the rest of the enclosure at 70°F (21°C).
RECOMMENDED KEEPING OUTSIDE IN SUMMER	Always; cold frame or greenhouse in the outdoor pen	Usually; cold frame or greenhouse in combination with pond setup	Usually; generally with cold frame in the outdoor pen (swampy landscape)
HIBERNATION REQUIRED	Always; wintering box in floor of greenhouse; refrigerator	Usually; wintering tank in aquarium at low temperature; refrigerator	Usually; often possible in terrarium at low temperature
ESTIVATION	Possible	Possible	Possible
ACCESSORIES IN TERRARIUM	UV and spotlights	UV and spotlights, also bright light and heat filter	UV and spotlights, humidity control often needed
PURCHASE PRICE	High	Fairly low, especially with large animals	High
NUTRITIONAL BASIS	Grasses and hay	Animal protein, with age also plant foods	Assorted foods
COMMERCIAL FOODS AVAILABLE	Hay pellets, but only as supplement	Thawed frozen food (crustaceans, fish, mice, insects) as supplementary diet; food pellets	Thawed frozen food (crustaceans, fish, mice, insects) as supplementary diet; food pellets
FRESH FOODS	Herbs, greens, and fruit (see Standard Mix, p. 48)	Crickets, white fish, water fleas, snails, earthworms	Snails, earthworms, herbs (see Standard Mix, p. 48)

Body Structure and Sense Organs

Ears

A turtle's sense of hearing is not very well developed. Low frequencies (deep tones) are perceived through both the ear and the arch of the carapace. The eardrum is the round structure in the center of the photo.

Eyes

The eye recognizes objects (food, enemies) very well at a distance. Up close, though, the vision is not very sharp. The sensitive cornea is protected by a pair of lids with a pronounced upper lid and kept moist by tear glands and the Harderian gland.

Nose

The sense of smell is very well developed, and it leads the turtle reliably to food and a mate. It takes over orienteering close to the object, where the eyes see only a blur. Aquatic turtles have a keen sense of smell under water. There are temperature-sensitive cells in the area around the nose and on the head.

Scales

Tortoises (top) have strong scales on their legs; these provide solid protection when the limbs are drawn in. An aquatic turtle's skin (bottom) has only small scales and is more elastic.

Carapace

The carapace or upper shell, gets its shape from dermal bones, which grow together with the ribs and extensions of the spinal column into a load-bearing arch. The dermal bones are between the colored scales and the bone.

A Tortoise's Legs

The legs have solid, cone-shaped claws that grow continually. The front feet are flattened (illustration), and the hind feet are round like pillars. The "finger joints" are inside the extremities. Temperature-sensing cells on the soles of the feet facilitate locating the desired ground temperature.

A Pond Turtle's Legs

They have movable finger joints with sharp, curved claws. There is webbing between them.

What Kind of Turtle Is Right for Me?

Before you decide on a specific species, you should ask yourself a few basic questions and be able to answer them in the affirmative. That way, you become aware of the responsibility you are taking on and the costs associated with it.

A Green Light for Owning a Turtle?

⟩ When you say *yes* to owning a turtle, you take on a long-term commitment. Are you prepared for this? After all, aquatic turtles and tortoises have a life expectancy between 60 and 120 years.

⟩ Along with a stand and the technical accessories, an aquarium that holds 55 to 110 gallons (200–400 l) weighs 550 to almost 1,000 pounds (250–450 kg) when filled with water. Then there is a load of over 220 pounds (100 kg) on each of the four legs of the stand, and that produces small pressure points that can damage the floor. Is the construction of your apartment able to withstand this? (Cement floors generally have no problem with this weight.) Is your landlord comfortable with this amount of water in the apartment?

⟩ In order to satisfy current requirements for living conditions, many turtle species are kept in the yard during the summer. Once a European tortoise or a terrapin reaches a shell length of 4 to 5 inches (10–12 cm) it belongs outdoors. Ideally it is kept in a secure outdoor pen or a pond – with a greenhouse in either case–or at least in a setup on a terrace or a balcony. Can you offer your animal this perceived "luxury," which merely satisfies the need for natural light conditions, physical exercise, and natural foraging?

⟩ I recommend beginners keep a single animal. But if you want to keep a mating pair, it is very important to know that pairs often are incompatible for most of the year. Can you recognize the behaviors that show that the animals are not tolerating one another? And are you then prepared to set up a second aquarium or terrarium for the partner?

⟩ Can you afford the ongoing costs for electricity, food, and medical treatments?

⟩ Are you prepared to sacrifice a half-day if necessary to get good veterinary care if there is no adequate help available in your area?

Not All Species Are a Good Choice

Appropriate for Beginners For beginning turtle hobbyists, I recommend only species that are bred in our latitudes. It's best to stick with ones that can be bred easily, for it is simpler to satisfy their needs.

Inappropriate for Beginners Large species and those that are known to be "fussy" keepers are

---

Space Requirements

LOTS OF ROOM Some smaller species have a need for large space because they are especially lively. If you want to get a species that is not mentioned in this manual, first look into it carefully.

NOT MUCH ROOM Many aquatic turtles are "lurkers" and don't need much room, e.g., the Mata Mata (*Chelus fimbriatus*). But that does not make them a good choice for beginners.

1 European Tortoises are active during the day. Because of their compulsion to move around, they need lots of room, and in the long run, an outdoor pen with a greenhouse.

2 The Spotted Turtle (*Clemmys guttata*), like the Striped Mud Turtle, is a small species at around 4 inches (10 cm) long. Both are active during the day and get along fine.

3 Side-necked turtles such as the Red-bellied Short-necked Turtle reach a size of 8 to 12 inches (20–30 cm). They are active during the day, need plenty of swimming room, and can live in the yard during the summer.

4 The Common Musk Turtle (Stinkpot) remains small (ca. 4 inches/10 cm), can be kept entirely in an aquarium, and is active only in the morning and the evening.

kept by many turtle hobbyists, but they often need sufficient room in an enclosure, a room to themselves in the house, and a wealth of experience on the part of the caregiver. Beginners should thus steer clear of the following species, even though they are available on the market: Common Snapping Turtle (*Chelydra serpentina*) 18½ inches (47 cm), up to 48 pounds (22 kg); Yellow-footed Tortoise (*Geochelone denticulata*), up to 24 inches (60 cm), maximum weight unknown; Leopard Tortoise (*Geochelone pardalis*), 31 inches (60 cm), up to 66 pounds (30 kg); African Spurred Tortoise (*Geochelone sulcata*), 31 inches (80 cm), up to 132 pounds (60 kg); Alligator Snapping Turtle (*Macrochelgs temminckii*), 27½ inches (70 cm), up to 220 pounds (100 kg); the female of the three Sliders (*Pseudemys* species), the Florida Cooter (*P. floridana*), River Cooter (*P. concinna*), and the Florida Red-bellied Cooter (*P. nelsoni*); they can reach a shell length of up to 15¾ inches (40 cm).

Species That Remain Small

Turtles can take up lots of space in your house or yard. If you do not have a yard, I recommend species that remain small and can be kept year-round in an aquarium. These include such species as the Striped Mud Turtle and the Common Musk Turtle (see pp. 22 ff.).

Species That Are Active at Dusk and at Night

Also consider if you have time in the morning and evening to take care of your turtle if you are gone all day. Then it would be advantageous to have a species that sleeps through the day and is active only in the morning and evening hours when you are home. Candidates for this are the Eastern Box Turtle and the Common Musk Turtle (see pp. 21 and 23).

Hibernation Basics

In the profiles section (pages 20 ff.) you will find information on whether the named species are candidates for hibernation. Many remain active throughout the year, such as the Red-bellied Short-necked Turtle. Still, there are some animals that may or may not hibernate, based on their distribution in their native habitat. These include the Common Musk Turtle and the Striped Mud Turtle. You can tell by its behavior in the autumn if a turtle wants to hibernate (see page 56).

1 When the leaves fall in the autumn, a European Tortoise stops eating and digs in. Thus begins its hibernation.

2 In the spring it comes out spontaneously as long as the temperature stays over 57–61°F (14–16° C). It makes up for lost water by drinking a lot.

Estivation Many turtles often sleep for weeks without food intake in the hot, dry summer months—they estivate. An Eastern Box Turtle, for example, digs into the earth, and a Striped Mud Turtle disappears into the sediment of its water. At this time leave your turtle in peace until it becomes active again of its own accord.

The Most Common Questions

Which species hibernate? The Eastern Box Turtle does not always hibernate, and with some species, such as the Striped Mud Turtle and the Common Musk Turtle, the need for hibernation depends on where the creature originally came from. It is important that you do not try to hibernate unless you know the point of origin. The farther north the origin, the greater the probability that the turtle will sleep through the winter. For more, see Tortoise Trust's "Safer Hibernation and Your Tortoise" at *www.tortoisetrust.org/articles/safer.html.*

How long does hibernation last in the wild? The length of hibernation depends on the species and origin of the turtle. Turtles whose homes are farther north hibernate longer than turtles from warmer, more southerly regions. Conversely, animals from more southerly latitudes are quicker to resume activity.

Where are the winter quarters located? A turtle can spend the winter in a space that is kept at 39–43°F (4–6°C). But this should temporarily be warmed up to 48°F (9°C), as it sometimes happens under natural conditions in the winter (see page 56).

Spending the Winter in the Cellar

Tortoises move into a special hibernation box that reproduces the natural conditions in a hiding place in the soil. The box is filled one quarter full with expanded clay for moisture retention, and another quarter full with forest soil, and the top half with dried beech or oak leaves. A plastic liner between the dirt and the clay will keep the turtle from digging down that far. Rising capillary water from the damp expanded clay will keep the hibernation environment at 80 to 90% relative humidity, without making things wet for the tortoise. Make sure your cellar is cool and can be maintained in the lower 40s. You might be able to use your garage as well. (See the Tortoise Trust's Website.)

Aquatic turtles are put into a plastic pan filled with enough water so that the animal can comfortably get air when it lies on the bottom (see illustration lower right). Oak leaves take the place of the sediment in the natural waters, and their tannin inhibits germ growth. A board is used to keep light from getting into the basin.

Hibernating in the Refrigerator

Instead of using a box in the cellar, turtles can also spend the winter in the vegetable drawer in the refrigerator.

You can bury your tortoise—right side up— in a transparent container filled with bark mulch or beech leaves. It should be at least as large as a shoe box. A good choice is a plastic container measuring about 17 × 13 × 9¼″ (43 × 33 × 23.5 cm) with a matching lid. Make holes in side walls of the box with a 5⁄16″ (8 mm) drill—one hole every 2½ inches or so (6–7 cm)—and attach a moist sponge the size of a box of matches under the lid (it must never touch the tortoise). That way you keep the humidity between 80 and 90%. Check it with a hygrometer and make sure that nothing is getting moldy.

You can likewise put your aquatic turtle into a plastic box in which the water is filled halfway with oak leaves (the water level is as described for the mortar pan). The box should be at least 50% wider and longer than the length of the turtle's shell. The animal must be able to turn around easily inside the box. It must not be able to reach the lid with fully outstretched neck. This air space serves as a storage area for breathing air, even though the need is greatly reduced during hibernation. Drill a few air holes above the water line in the side walls of airtight boxes, as described for tortoises.

3 Tropical species do not hibernate. The Red-bellied Short-necked Turtle does, however, appreciate a temperature reduction of a few degrees (2°C) from November through February.

4 Terrapins hibernate among oak leaves in still water and total darkness. But they must be able to get air at the surface at any time.

Testudo hermanni boettgeri
Hermann's Tortoise

   10 inches (25 cm)

Distribution Greece, Turkey, Romania, Bulgaria, Albania, Serbia, and Croatia. Alluvial forests, shady brush lands with water holes.

Living Conditions Young animals in a terrarium at least 4 feet square (1.2 m²). Outdoors in the summer. When shell reaches length of 3 to 4 inches (8–10 cm), outdoors year round with greenhouse. Ground temperature 68–73°F (20–23°C), air temperature 64–79°F (18–26°C), plus heat lamp at 113°F (45°C); also in greenhouse. Provide cover for young animals.

Behavior Active in early morning and late afternoon. Likes to climb and dig.

Miscellaneous Pronounced horn spike on tip of tail and (usually) a divided tail scute. Avoid purchasing hybrids of Hermann's and Greek tortoises.

Reproduction Very good breeding results. Females reach sexual maturity at about 10 to 14 years, males at 5 to 7 years. Clutch of three to eight eggs starting in the spring, up to three clutches per season. Incubation period 2 to 3 months.

Testudo marginata
Marginated Tortoise

   12 to 14 inches (30–35 cm)

Two subspecies: *T. m. marginata, T. m. weissingeri*.
Distribution Greece, southern peninsula. The animals prefer karst slopes in dry regions (shrub land).

Living Conditions Young animals in a terrarium at least 4 square feet (1.2 m²). Outdoors in the summer. Outdoors year round with a greenhouse once shell length reaches 3 to 4 inches (8–10 cm). Ground temperature 68–73°F (20–23°C), air temperature 64°F (18°C) (nighttime) up to 81°F (27°C) during the day, plus heat lamp at 113°F (45°C); also in greenhouse. Provide cover for young animals.

Behavior Active in early morning and later afternoon. Likes to climb and dig.

Miscellaneous The largest European tortoise. Carapace with curved rear edge.

Reproduction Very good breeding results. Two clutches per season possible with three to eight eggs. Incubation period 2 to 3 months. For breeding purposes avoid buying hybrids of Greek and Marginated Tortoises.

❄ Hibernation   ☀ Diurnal   🔅 Active at Dusk   〰 In Open Water   🏕 Lives on Land Near Water

Testudo graeca

Greek Tortoise

  10 to 12 inches (25–30 cm)

Approx. six subspecies

Distribution Northern Africa, southern Spain, the Balearic Islands, Sardinia, southeastern Europe, Armenia, Turkey, East Caucasus and Iran. Steppes, brush land, dry forests, semi-deserts, and cropland.

Living Conditions Young animals in a terrarium at least 4 square feet (1.2 m²). Outdoors in the summer. Outdoors year round once shell length reaches 3 to 4 inches (8–10 cm). Ground temperature 72–77°F (22–25°C), air temperature 68°F (20°C) (night) to 82°F (28°C), plus heat lamp at 113°F (45°C), also in greenhouse. Likes warmth.

Behavior Lively; digs well.

Miscellaneous Horn cone near upper thigh. In the wild, hibernates for 6 to 7 months. Estivation possible. Animals of origin outside Europe are not suited to beginners.

Reproduction One to three clutches per season with four to eight eggs each, usually in the morning. Hatch after 2 to more than 3 months.

Terrapene carolina

Eastern Box Turtle

   4 to 7 inches (10–18 cm)

Six subspecies: *T. c. carolina, T. c. major,* and *T. c. triunguis* are often found for sale.

Distribution USA, except in the West. Rather moist forest areas and meadows.

Living Conditions Terrarium at least 4 square feet (1.2 m²) and outdoor pen with heated greenhouse. Ground temperature 68–79°F (20–26°C), air temperature near ground 68°C (20°C) at night and up to 82°F (28°C) during the day; also spotlight at 104–113°F (40–45°C). Except for *T. c. triunguis,* sensitive to dry air under 70% humidity. Deep swimming basin. Access to UV and daylight.

Behavior Likes morning and evening sun; likes to lie for hours or days in the water. In dry periods, digs in for weeks.

Miscellaneous "Land-dwelling terrapin"; *T. c. carolina* grows to only 6 ¼ inches (16 cm); *T. c. major* likes to swim and lives near the water; *T. c. triunguis* prefers a rather dry habitat.

Reproduction Not much breeding; avoid hybrids.

 Amphibious Near Shoreline   ❉ Plant Food   Mixed Food   Meat

Emydura subglobosa

Red-bellied Short-necked Turtle

   7 inches (18 cm)

Two subspecies: *E. s. subglobosa, E. s. worrellii.*
Distribution Southern New Guinea and the northern tip of Australia (Cape York; Jardine River).
Living Conditions In protected outdoor pen only in hot peak of summer; otherwise, year round in an aquarium with lots of room for swimming; at least 60 × 20 inches (150 × 50 cm) and 16 inches (40 cm) of water (= 83 gallons/300 l). Water temperature from November to February 77°F (25°C), otherwise 81°F (27°C). Air temperature during the day a few degrees higher than water temperature. For exclusive aquarium living provide UV and daylight.
Behavior Very good swimmer, rarely on land; shy.
Miscellaneous "Side-neck" protects head and neck by tucking them in to the side. Animals of Australian origin grow to 10 inches (25 cm) long.
Reproduction Very good breeding results. April to June about seven to ten eggs per clutch; multiple layings per year possible. Incubation period 6 to 7 weeks at 82°F (28°C).

Kinosternon baurii

Striped Mud Turtle

    4¾ inches (12 cm)

Two subspecies: *K. b. palmarum, K. b. bauri.*
Distribution Florida, southern Georgia.
Living Conditions Aquarium 3 feet long, 16 inches wide, and 20 inches high (1 m × 40 cm × 50 cm; = 55 gallons / 200 l); water depth 2 inches (5 cm) for young animals, maximum of 12 inches (30 cm) for adults. Fine sandy, soft bottom ¾ to 1 inch (20–25 mm); depending on genetic origin, water temperature 64–82°F (18–28°C). Land area 16 inches on a side (40 × 40 cm). Access to daylight required. Climbing aids and a basking place in the water with roots and sisal ropes.
Behavior Somewhat shy, calm. Climbs a lot underwater, also swims in a pinch.
Miscellaneous Two hinges on plastron. Males have horn spike on tip of tail. May not hibernate, depending on origin; may estivate.
Reproduction Rarely breeds. Sexually mature at 5 to 7 years. Clutch of one to eight eggs, successive clutches also possible. Hatch after 3 to 5 months.

Sternotherus odoratus

Common Musk Turtle

    3 inches (10 cm)

Distribution From southeastern Canada through the eastern United States down to Florida.

Living Conditions Singly in an aquarium, 40 inches long, 16 inches wide, and 20 inches high (100 cm × 40 cm × 50 cm). Water depth 4 to 6 inches (10–15 cm) for young animals, 10 to 12 inches (25–30 cm) for adults. Water temperature 77°F (25°C), air temperature 79–81°F (26–27°C). Rarely basks, and then usually right under the surface of the water. Daylight is adequate. One inch (2 cm) sand bottom. Climbing aids necessary; underwater hollows for hiding with easy access to surface.

Behavior Active at dusk; in hiding during the day. Walks on bottom and climbs to surface of water; not fond of swimming; rarely on land.

Miscellaneous Mating pairs must often be kept apart. Insatiable appetite; avoid overfeeding.

Reproduction Satisfactory breeding results. Clutch with two to four eggs; young hatch after 11 to 12 weeks and are no larger than ladybugs.

Emys orbicularis

European Pond Turtle

    10 inches (25 cm)

Thirteen subspecies, including *E. o. orbicularis* (Central Europe), *E. o. hellenica* (Po Lowlands, Balkans), *E. o. fritzjuergenobsti* (Spain).

Distribution Central and southern Europe, the Balkans, northwestern Africa.

Living Conditions Avoid keeping year round in an aquarium. Water area at least 4 by 20 inches and 16 inches deep (120 cm × 50 cm × 40). Water temperature 72–75°F (22–24°), air temperature 79–82°F (26–38°C). Provide UV and daylight. Can be kept in yard once shell length reaches 3 inches (8 cm). Two ponds for a mating pair.

Behavior Swims well, likes to bask on the land; sometimes remains shy.

Miscellaneous Outside the mating season, generally keep female separated from male.

Reproduction Very good breeding results. Starting at the age of 10, possible egg laying from June on at a depth of approx. 4 inches (10 cm). Incubation period scarcely 3 months.

 Amphibious Near Shoreline   Plant Food   Mixed Food   Meat

Where Do I Get a Turtle?

Before you decide on a species, use this manual to select one that is a good match for you. Then find out if and where there are study groups or other organizations that deal with the species you have chosen (see page 62 for suggestions). Also ask them for the addresses of owners in your area.

Where and When to Buy

Where to Buy You can get turtles from dealers, who generally sell offspring from private parties, or

directly from the breeder. A good dealer can answer questions about the animal's feeding, species, and age, as well as basic requirements for living conditions, and certainly will have no problem producing any documentation required by local or national species protection legislation (see page 10). Buying from a breeder comes with an extra benefit: you get a direct look at a functioning turtle setup and the animal's requirements in technical accessories and space. Never buy a turtle from vacation bazaars, flea markets, or the Internet.

When to Buy It is best to buy between May and August, for then any hibernation is over, and you have time to get the turtle used to living with you and to check its health. This is very critical with purchases in the autumn. You will not recognize an illness, and the turtle will go into hibernation with it and will probably die in hibernation. If you purchase a turtle too early, say in March or April, you cannot be certain that the animal did not fall ill during hibernation and that the illness will first manifest itself at your house. Carefully inspect the animal you want to buy (see page 54).

Consider Carefully At this point please take my urgent advice to heart about carefully weighing the pros and cons of buying a turtle. Species in which the females reach 8 to 12 inches (20–30 cm)— including many of the painted turtles and cooters— can often be obtained for free as adults from

Young animals like to gather in a secure hiding place (remote in this case). When they are older, they become loners.

animal homes, zoos, and animal rescue organizations. There the animals, which were allowed to "run free" by their former owners, contrary to species protection principles, are cared for. Giving away turtles rarely happens spontaneously; more often that not it occurs after a careful search for a new care provider. Simply letting the animals go in the wild goes against regulations and amounts to cruelty to animals.

Buying from a Breeder

When you buy an animal from a breeder, you will not only learn about the species but also be able to ask about the precise living conditions. This is especially helpful with species that are widely distributed, as in the case of the Common Musk Turtle and the European Pond Turtle. That way you can get relatively accurate advice about your animal's preferred temperature range and need for hibernation.

Old or Young Turtle?

Young animals from domestic breeders require particularly careful, skilled feeding and care. This is the only way for a young turtle to grow up healthy and without shell deformities. It is easier to acclimate a half-grown animal starting at age 3 than a grown turtle with a hardened bone structure. There is certainly nothing wrong with adopting a healthy adult animal that someone else has kept for a long time. Then there is also practically no doubt about the eventual size.

Male or Female?

Many males from the mentioned aquatic turtle species generally remain smaller than the females (see p. 22 ff.). So if you don't have lots of available room for an aquarium or a terrarium, it's better to choose a male. By the same token, you should consider whether you will want to have several animals later on: you cannot keep two males—or generally even a mating pair—together permanently. Keeping two females from the same species, on the other hand, may work out well. After two or three years of experience with your turtle you can evaluate the risk yourself.

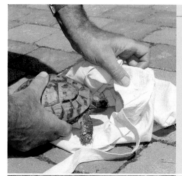

1 For transporting a fairly large turtle, you can put it into a breathable cloth bag made from nettle cloth with the seams on the outside. Then it can be put into a box.

2 Plastic transport containers are appropriate for young animals, especially aquatic turtles, which are always transported in damp, clean paper towels, not floating in water.

The Way Turtles Live

Turtles actively regulate their body temperature by searching out and assuming the appropriate temperature in their surroundings. The terrarium must therefore satisfy the basic need for the preferred temperature. This chapter will show you the other things that it must also provide.

What Turtles Need

Size accounts for only part of the quality of a turtle installation. The way it is set up is just as important. The following basic rules apply to all the setups described in this manual.

Providing Warming and Cooling

A turtle uses its warmth sensors to locate places that provide warmth from the outside. This is particularly important in the morning to get the animal up to speed, and in the afternoon for digesting food. Even turtles that are active at dusk often bask in the early morning. If it gets too hot for the animals, tortoises cool off in the shade, and aquatic turtles temporarily dive into cooler areas of the water. Take this into consideration when you measure and set up your installation. If you provide a greenhouse for your charge, remember that night-time temperatures in February and March can dip below 53°F (12°C). You need to prevent this by regulating the heat. It's best to orient yourself by the temperature data provided in the Profiles section (see p. 20 ff).

A Good Substrate Is Important

The substrate should store both warmth and moisture and offer some rough stone slabs for tortoises to wear down their claws. Deciduous forest dirt, possibly mixed with bark mulch, is a good floor for storing moisture and for digging. Loessic and loamy soils (from a garden store) are good for setting up appropriate sections of dry ground under the spotlight. Once it hardens and becomes smooth, it is very easy to keep clean. It also stores warmth well.

Requirements for the Turtle Installation

There are minimal requirements for providing the proper living conditions for animals. This includes the size of the terrarium. This manual's recommendations exceed the bare minimums so that your pet will have enough room to move around, and you will have plenty of opportunities to put in interesting and creative elements. These take up more room than you may think, and they reduce the open space for the turtle. On the other hand, the decoration provides an environment with variety that will motivate the turtle to wander about.

Around the **Turtle Installation**

PREVENT GLASS BREAKAGE Protect your all-glass aquarium or terrarium from breakage. Place the aquarium on an underlay that is perfectly flat and solid, and insert a thick piece of protective foam mat under the glass bottom of the aquarium. This will keep irregularities and grains of sand from causing the bottom to crack.

REUSE OLD AQUARIUMS Even if they are cracked or no longer waterproof, old aquariums can still be used as terrariums, since they don't need to contain water.

USE A MORTAR PAN FROM A HARDWARE STORE These simple, economical containers can be set up as quarantine quarters, for laying eggs, or as initial accommodations for young animals. Pans with a capacity of 27–33 gallons (100–120 l) are good choices.

The terrarium for tortoises does not need to be watertight, but it must always be well ventilated. The size depends on the expected average ultimate size of your tortoise, as specified in the Profiles section (see page 20 ff). A terrarium takes up lots of room, for a healthy tortoise needs sufficient area for wandering about.

An aquaterrarium for pond turtles consists of a waterproof aquarium with a large land portion. This should match the turtle's urge to move around and its expected final size. The water portion should be large enough so that the creature can dive under water and lie on the shore; however, in comparison to the land portion, the water portion should be smaller.

The aquarium for aquatic turtles needs a smaller land area than a terrarium does because the turtle can use the "third dimension," that is, the depth of the water. In addition, the land portion is used for laying eggs and basking out of the water and thus does not take up any area for swimming.

The Quarantine Station

A special quarantine container is always required, even when you have only one turtle. In case of illness it provides a better place for caring for your animal, for the tank is smaller and easier to keep clean. Young animals can also be put out in the yard in it (but don't forget partial shade and a mesh cover; see page 40 ff), so that they don't have to leave their home.

Young animals come in a container that may consist of a rectangular plastic mortar pan (from a hardware store) that contains 33 gallons (120 l).

A solarium offers ideal conditions with daylight, the increasing length of which throughout the year governs the turtle's biology. The terrarium must always be set up in such a way that it is bright, but without direct sunlight; it must be free from draft, tobacco smoke, and floor vibrations.

In accordance with the requirements for a terrarium, this is set up and brought to the appropriate temperature. A ridge tile makes a good shelter for all species. Aquatic turtles can climb onto it when they want to leave the water.

For temporary stays, **adult animals** need containers that are about half as large as the terrariums recommended in the Profiles section. The water level for turtles that walk under water, such as the Musk and the Striped Mud Turtles, must be the equivalent of one shell width (straight measurement, without taking into account the curvature of the shell). For good swimmers, such as Red-bellied Short-necked Turtles and Pond Turtles, the water level should equal at least twice the breadth of the shell. In this instance, deeper water is better.

Light

The well-being and health of your turtle are highly dependent on the extent to which you can provide light conditions that are as natural as possible by means of technical aids. The installation is never totally illuminated. There must always be a darker corner to which the turtles can retreat.

The fluorescent daylight tube provides the basic lighting that is always required in a deficiency of natural daylight (e.g., in a dark corner of the room). It also helps the plants thrive, and it is con-

trolled by a timer. The daily duration of lighting is oriented to the current length of the day.

A spotlight provides the "warmth of the sun" and is always necessary. It is operated by a timer switch during the turtle's active period. At a distance of 3 feet (1 m) a 100-watt spotlight with a ten-degree diffusion angle produces a light spot about 7 inches (17 cm) in diameter and a light intensity of 10,000 lux. Save some energy and try a 60-watt spotlight hung at about 8 inches (20 cm). It must reach 104–113°F (40–45°C) on the floor. For mud turtles (*Sternotherus, Kinosternon*), the spotlight also serves as an adequate light source.

The UV lamp is essential for indoor living and is also governed by a timer switch. It hangs about 2 feet (60 cm) over the installation and shines for about 20 minutes during the turtle's first activity period and for just 10 minutes during the second activity period. UV light (= sunlight) is extremely important for bone growth, and thus for shell and joints. Based on scientific research, I can recommend the 200-watt Ultra-Vitalux lamp type from Osram ("face tanner") or identical lamps from other manufacturers (Philipps, Sylvania). But the UV yield and supply of other types of lamp such as HQL or blended light lamps is not very reliable (see Books, page 62).

Halogen-metal vapor lamps (HQI-, HCI-, or HQI-TS lamps) mainly satisfy the requirements of *Emydura* and *Emys* species. But even tortoises that are kept indoors year-round need the bright light for remaining vital. Consider using quartz (HQI) and ceramic (HCI) bulbs. They produce 13,000 lumens at 150 watts, thus coming close to daylight. In

1 The spotlight is the turtle's heat source. It is controlled by a timer switch. Outdoors it is protected from precipitation by a metal reflector.

2 An HQI-TS lamp is as bright as day and has a positive effect on the turtle's vitality. It can also be installed above the installation.

addition, ceramic bulbs last longer than quartz bulbs. Also, they do not change their spectrum through long usage, in contrast to HQI bulbs.

Taking the Current Length of the Day into Account

I recommend that you conform to the light intensity of the season by placing the HQI lamp about 30 inches (80 cm) above the installation during the summer, and raising it to about 5 feet (1.5 m) in the spring and fall. This corresponds to the varying intensity of the sun, which in our latitudes is much higher in the middle of summer than in the spring and the fall.

Health Advantages The changing length of the days is tremendously important for the turtle's health. The shortening days in the fall control the animal's inner clock and use a hormonal change to produce a decrease in metabolism, an adjustment in food intake, and an emptying of the digestive system. It would be harmful for the animal if you failed to observe the current length of the day and instead kept up a consistent lighting duration into the winter, thereby interfering with your turtle's hibernation.

Individual Light Requirements Mud turtles that are active in the twilight have different light needs than sun-hungry species that are active during the day. For them, it is sufficient to perceive from under the water how the length of the days is changing. The intensity of the light is a secondary consideration. But try to observe—especially in the morning—whether your turtle continues to seek out the UV and heat lamps.

Regulating **UV Light**

TIPS FROM
TURTLE EXPERT
Dr. Hartmut Wilke

UV RAYS PENETRATE WATER Fifty percent of the ultraviolet rays that fall on the surface penetrate through 8 inches (20 cm) of clean aquarium water. When you observe your aquatic turtle there, it basks and indicates a corresponding need.

UV RAYS HAVE NO EFFECT BEHIND GLASS The part of the UV spectrum (UV-B ray) that is important for bone growth cannot get through glass, fairly old Plexiglas, and polycarbonate sheets—from which cold frames and greenhouses are made. This can be offset by keeping the turtle outdoors or using a UV lamp.

VITAMIN D_3 DROPS ARE NO SUBSTITUTE On the contrary, an overdose could poison your pet.

TOO MUCH UV IS POINTLESS If the daily exposure of a turtle to a UV lamp at a distance of 24 to 30 inches (60–80 cm) is longer than 10 to 20 minutes, there is no bonus for health. Further exposure merely breaks down the initial level of vitamin D_3.

Temperature

Turtles need access to warmer and cooler areas as needed. This is not a problem for tortoises because of the availability of sunny and shady places in the wild or in a spacious outdoor pen. The same applies to aquatic turtles when they discover sections of water at different temperatures in a large backyard pond. It is more difficult to offer these different temperature zones in an indoor installation, however.

Tortoises Even though the Profile section specifies narrow temperature ranges in which a turtle is active, that does not mean the entire terrarium should be at those temperatures. It is much better to consider these as empirical values that approximate the preferred body temperature. And a tortoise must be able to achieve them—by changing from warm to cold and vice-versa. A terrarium with various temperature zones is ideal.

A terrarium for tortoises has a gradient for temperature and bottom moisture. Concentrate the lamps on the warmer, dry side and be mindful of walkways and a swimming area.

Aquatic Turtles Mud turtles that are active at dusk, particularly *Kinosternon* and *Sternotherus*, must achieve their preferred temperature in the body of water where they live. However, *Emys* and *Emydura* can also bask outside the water, for they are active during the day. But do not underestimate the variety of temperatures that a natural body of water offers. The water in calm, sunny shore areas and right under the surface is significantly warmer than at a depth of 8 inches (20 cm) or more. Similarly, turtles can warm themselves more effectively and for a longer time in calm water zones than in areas of flowing water.

Setting Up a Temperature Gradient In order to meet your turtle's temperature requirements as completely as possible, I recommend that you keep the animal in a spacious, elongated terrarium. That will make it easy to provide the required temperature gradient—we also speak in terms of a "temperature organ"—and your pet can seek warmer or cooler zones at will (see illustration at left).

Indications of Hibernation

At the same time, providing areas of varying warmth in the terrarium has a further advantage. They make it easier for you to find out when your tortoise is ready for hibernation. At a given time, it will withdraw into a cooler corner and dig in. Now you should immediately start the preparations for hibernation (see page 19). With aquatic turtles, the readiness for hibernation is not as easy to recognize. You can find information on which species hibernate and what water temperatures are required in the Profile section (see page 22 ff.) and on page 56 ff.

Preventing Health Issues

TIPS FROM
TURTLE EXPERT
Dr. Hartmut Wilke

HEAT BUILDUP The top of the installation should be wide open so that there is no heat buildup from the spotlights. The heat escapes unhindered from open installations, and cooler air flows in. This also applies to sunbathers in a mortar pan (see page 28).

IMPROPER WATER TEMPERATURE If your aquatic turtle suddenly leaves the water for hours or days, make sure the water temperature is correct. A malfunctioning water heater allows the water to cool off quickly, and the turtle will seek warmth on land.

COLD AIR Make sure that the air is always a few degrees warmer than the water. If it becomes colder, your aquatic turtle could suffer health consequences (see page 53).

EXCESSIVELY COLD FLOOR If the floor of the terrarium is significantly colder than 64°F (18°C), you can install an electrical heating pad according to the manufacturer's instructions. Set the thermostat to 64°F (18°C) in order to prevent growth abnormalities, such as a deformed shell, which often occur at higher pad temperatures.

The Right Climate

In addition to light and temperature, other factors, such as humidity play a role. Even aquatic turtles are dependent on this when they lay their eggs on land or seek winter quarters, as with the Musk Turtle.

A Comfortable Habitat in the Terrarium

The proper humidity is of great importance for tortoises. Most European species are comfortable

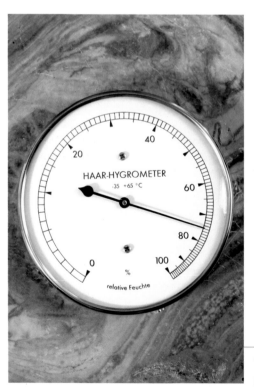

at 60 to 70%, but two subspecies of the Eastern Box Turtle (see page 21) need humidity no lower than 70% because their organism is adapted to humid environments. Neither skin nor lungs can tolerate dry air for very long, and it can damage both. Since they require care from very experienced hands, I do not recommend them for beginning turtle owners.

The right ground moisture is easy to provide if you use deciduous forest dirt as a substrate. It absorbs water well, is loose, and is also good for digging. If your pet eats it—often because of a mineral deficiency—the dirt can pass through the digestive tract. Sand or gravel, on the other hand, accumulates in the intestine and can lead to death from constipation. Substrates with a higher density, which turtles prefer for laying eggs, can be made by combining deciduous forest dirt and sand in even proportions.

Maintaining Ambient Humidity You can use various measures to provide the appropriate humidity in the terrarium:
> The swimming basin merely serves to provide the turtle's immediate need for moisture. The animal will lie in it for 10 to 20 minutes and absorb moisture through the skin or by drinking. The evaporation of the water does not contribute to an increase in humidity, however, because it is too insignificant. Incidentally, staying in the water for hours at a time may be a symptom of illness.

The Haar hygrometer indicates the humidity as a percentage. It is very precise and needs no batteries.

› You can use a plant mister to keep the ground "misty damp," but you must never saturate it. Go over it until even the lower layers remain uniformly moist.

› Plants are helpful in raising the humidity, for they transpire water through their surface. They still must be sprayed daily and watered regularly.

› A pane of glass used to partially cover the terrarium helps to keep the humidity inside as long as possible. But make sure this does not produce any heat accumulation (see page 33). Do not place the pane of glass over the heated area, and of course never use it when the spotlights and heating lamp are turned on. But after that time the glass will prevent further drying out. Never cover the terrarium completely. Slight air circulation must always be possible, and it must never smell musty.

› A type of "waterfall" can satisfy the great need for moisture with such species as the Eastern Box Turtle. With help from a low-power aquarium pump, the waterfall flows over a piece of pond liner hanging on the inside of the glass and then drips into the basin. The liner must be washed off, and the water must be changed every two days; otherwise, musty smelling slime fungi suddenly develop.

A Comfortable Habitat in the Aquarium

Water quality is crucial for the proper climate in an aquarium. You need a heat filter, which you use on a low setting according to the manufacturer's instructions to produce just a mild current. It cleans and warms the water at the same time. Inside the aquarium, the drain is fitted with a commercially produced wire guard, and the water change, which occurs every 7 to 14 days, is facilitated by a valve on the bottom. Wash the body of the filter—usually foam—in cold water every 4 to 6 weeks.

An electric heating wand needs a protective basket to ensure that the heating element does not break and to keep the turtle from getting burned on it.

The substrate can consist of fine, soft sand. It is only ⅜ to ⅝" (1–1.5 cm) deep, should be non-reflective, and also looks attractive. The finer the substrate is, the less waste accumulates in the gaps and the easier it is to keep clean. If your turtle eats it, which happens very rarely, you can replace the sand with a piece of commercially produced artificial turf (plastic, no felt); this is also easier to clean.

Setting Up a Terrarium

A tortoise places a few demands on its home: It needs lots of exercise, cover for the night, a shallow swimming basin with an adjacent warm basking place, and a damp corner for digging, which a female can also use for laying eggs. In addition to the size, the inside setup of a terrarium will determine whether your tortoise feels comfortable. The way in which you decorate it is crucial. In planning the setup, use the information on the origin and behavior of the individual species (see p. 20 ff).

Interior Fittings and Design

Hiding places can be small, but not so tight that the creature can get stuck. You can keep this from happening by using a soft floor. The tortoise should always have the ability to climb around or away from obstacles.

The water basin is keyed to the size of the tortoise, which should be able to fit in comfortably with legs outstretched. The water level should reach only to the base of the tortoise's neck (just over the lower shell or plastron). The inner edge slopes gently so even young animals can climb out easily. Similarly, the basin needs a comfortable access from the land side. Place some sandstone slabs on the shore; their abrasive effect will keep the claws short.

The feeding area consists of a stone slab that is larger than the adult tortoise. It should not lie directly under the spotlight. Important: especially in a large terrarium, a young animal should be fed immediately in front of its hiding place, for it will be reluctant to leave it.

You can place **roots and stones** in such a way that they also create a cave for the night. Make sure that large stones are placed securely. Otherwise, a plate of glass can quickly be broken when a tortoise knocks one over while climbing and digging. This also applies to the vegetation.

Opportunities to keep busy, such as digging and climbing or poking around curiously with eyes and nose, should challenge your pet every day. Create open surfaces in the form of a figure-eight, in which the two loops of the eight each contain a hill with vegetation. This will offer your pet an interesting walking route. Remember that at first shy animals will be reluctant to leave their hiding place. Wait patiently for your pet to appear of its own accord.

Choosing the **Right Plants**

IN NURSERIES, you can get good advice on the types of plants that are best suited to your installation. Watch for chemically treated plants, however!

REFERENCE BOOKS provide precise directions on care and warnings about poisonous plants.

ARTIFICIAL PLANTS are often beguiling and easy to care for; however, they contribute nothing to the climate in the terrarium.

APPROPRIATE SETUP Large terrariums are best for setting up in an appropriate, decorative, and interesting manner. They offer a tortoise sunny, dry places, plus shady, moist hiding places. In searching for food and appropriate temperatures, it must wander around and climb several times a day. Under these conditions, exclusive indoor living is acceptable for certain species. The installation's large volume allows stable climate regulation.

NATURALISTIC DECORATING You can create the most beautiful design, which will also enrich your home, with decorating materials from nature. You can mirror a slice of nature with solid rocks and branches. Still, you must leave enough open space for the needs of an adult tortoise. Purely for reasons of daily cleaning, the drinking bowl is freestanding.

SKILLFUL PLANTING Arrange the vegetation in the terrarium in such a way that your tortoise cannot reach the greenery. That will keep your plants from getting eaten.

Setting Up an Aquarium

Good swimmers among the aquatic turtles need considerable open swimming room, an extensive land portion, and a secure hiding place that covers them from above. Often they use the suspended land portion, when they can brace themselves on a root or a stone below it. The animals also enjoy drifting on the surface.

Mud Turtles like to rest on supporting underwater structures and wait for food that comes drifting by. They have also been known to use a root that sticks out of the water for basking. In jumping from the basking place into deep water—like all aquatic turtles—the animal must not be allowed to hit its shell on the bottom. So be sure that the water is sufficiently deep.

Making Hiding Places Available

The creatures like pieces of dry reeds and dried leaves, cattails, or pine bark (flotsam) resting on the water's surface. These collect into small islands that provide floating turtles with cover and give the water a natural look. Water plants are even better; they can also serve as food, and especially in the case of meat eaters such as Mud Turtles (see page 22), they can last a long time. As described for tortoises, decorating with plants is best when done outside the aquarium.

Organizing the Land Portion

The land portion serves for basking and laying eggs. For this purpose both the land portion and the approach are warmed to 104–113°F (40–45°C).

Appearance The land portion should be around two to three times longer than your turtle's shell.

The turtle must be able to turn around and have the option of positioning itself sideways with respect to the heating point of the spotlight. The bottom is filled with an equal mixture of sand and deciduous forest dirt to a depth of 1½ times the length of the shell. Make sure that the approach to the land portion is at a gentle slope and secure. But the side walls must be high enough so that the turtle can leave it only in the direction of the water.

Installation To preserve ample swimming room, install the land portion over the surface of the water. It may stick into the water for a distance of an inch or two (3–5 cm) as long as the turtle cannot get stuck under it. Hang the land portion from ⅛ inch glued Plexiglas sheets or commercially available plastic containers with 5/64 to ⅛ inch (2–3 mm) of clearance between the glass panes in two stainless steel hangers (from a locksmith). On both ends the two hangers, grip the edge of the glass of the aquarium (with foam padding).

Cork for **Decoration**

VERSATILE   Pieces of cork tubing provide a secure hideout, and in sheet form they make good ramps for climbing out of the water and for basking.

ALWAYS ATTACH SECURELY   The cork must be attached to the rim of the tank with wire so that it does not sway when the turtle walks on it. This is especially true for "floating islands."

CLIMBING AIDS A large cork tube is an ideal decorative item for a turtle aquarium. It is natural, and the coarse surface facilitates climbing. Because of its insulating properties, it does not draw away through the lower shell the warmth that the turtle gets under the spotlight. So the turtle can warm up more quickly than in the water. The inside of the tube offers poor swimmers an ideal hiding place near the surface of the water.

A BASKING SPOT Not all turtles enjoy basking on the shore. There they feel secure only if—in case of danger—they can leave the spot with a single turn and dive into deep water. If the shore is made up of stone or gravel, use a thermometer to make sure that the subsoil is about 104°F (40°C), and if necessary, adjust the height of the spotlight.

WALKWAY In an outdoor pen, install a steady log for basking and as a way to get out of the water. Here it is clearly visible so that the turtle can stay close to the water for safety reasons.

A Sensible Outdoor Enclosure Design

The outdoor enclosure is set up in such a way that the morning and afternoon sun shines on it; day-long sunshine is ideal. In northern latitudes, outdoor pens without a greenhouse should be used by turtles only from June through August.

A Useful Setup

Vegetation Tortoises need bushes that provide shade and produce fruits (raspberries, currants, blackberries). Aquatic turtles cool off in the shade of cattails and reeds or in the deep water in the pond. Grassy areas are used as herb pastures—stores sell special turtle mixtures.

Decoration Tortoises like dirt hills for basking and use them to good advantage for catching the morning sun. Aquatic turtles store up warmth on the shore or on roots that stick up from the water. A swimming basin for tortoises, as in a terrarium, and an outlet for rainwater, which prevents flooding from rain, complete the outdoor pen.

Useful Precautions

Preventing Escapes All outdoor pens must be surrounded by an opaque palisade fence at least 16 inches (40 cm) high. My tip: walls store up heat for the night in combination with a greenhouse (see illustration at left). In hard soil, a stockade at least 1 foot (30 cm) deep will keep European tortoises from tunneling out. With soft, sandy ground, 20 inches (50 cm) is recommended. To keep the border visually acceptable, you can lower the level of the outdoor pen or pile up dirt along outside of the stockade. If children have access to your property, the pond must additionally be secured with a fence to prevent accidental drowning.

Keeping Out Enemies Beware of crows that sometimes peck out a turtle's eyes or fly away with the young. You can protect young turtles from such attack with nets or strings stretched over the outdoor installation. In small enclosures, you can use chicken wire for a cover. At night the turtles must be safe from raccoons, skunks, and cats. So close all the shutters and windows on the hiding place.

Designing a Pond

For an aquatic turtle, there is nothing better than life in a pond. But in northern latitudes, living outdoors is possible only from June through August. However, with the aid of a greenhouse, you can also use the spring and the late summer. For reasons of space, I provide here only an overview of the most important points for constructing a pond. If you then want to put one in, I recommend further reading in *My Turtle* (see Books, page 62).

Shape The pond should be round and have a broad, shallow shore area and a depth in the middle of about 3 feet (1 m). With a diameter of

about 20 feet (6 m), it will hold over 1,500 gallons (5,600 l) of water, of which almost 1,100 gallons (4,000 l) is in the shore area, where the water warms up quickly in the sun. Plant cattails or reeds in the center in a tub filled with sand, and place around this group some old logs out to the shallow water areas as basking islands. For a carnivorous mud turtle, you can plant the pond with *Egeria densa* or mouse-ear chickweed. But other turtle species will prefer any kind of greenery except for reeds and cattails.

Technical Accessories If there are no more than three turtles living in the pond described here, a filter is unnecessary, for the water will process the organic pollution from the animals. It may need cleaning in the center, though—where most of the waste collects—with the help of a submersible wastewater pump.

The outer wall of the greenhouse divides the outside portion of the pond from the inside. When it is cold out, the turtles swim into the warm interior.

41

Cold Frame and Greenhouse

In Greece, the homeland of many tortoises, the animals are active as early as February and sometimes can be found outdoors until the beginning of December. With an average temperature of about 68°F (20°C) and sparse precipitation, from May to June in Greece, it is about twice as warm as in more northerly climes, where an average of 50°F (10°C) is scarcely reached. This indicates that in comparison with the homeland of tortoises, our summers are too cool and wet. But you can avoid this shortcoming. Place your animal into a cold frame or a greenhouse, where it is possible to create a temperate climate even in bad weather. That way the turtle can remain active into November and emerge from hibernation as early as the end of February or the beginning of March.

A Cold Frame: Easy to Set Up

At about 3 feet on a side (1 m²), a cold frame is significantly smaller, cheaper, and easier to set up than a greenhouse. You can buy kits at garden stores. A cold frame serves turtles as a warm hiding place on cold days and during the night.

For tortoises it is easy to install the cold frame in the outdoor pen with the open back against a wall, for at night it provides storage for heat. It should be exposed to morning sun. Entry is gained through an opening with a slide closure or a commonly available cat door. You can easily use a jigsaw to cut the opening out of the Plexiglas or the double acrylic panes.

Aquatic turtles don't need a flap, for when it is set up appropriately on the shore, a quarter of their house sticks out into the water with the lower edge submerged. That way the animal can swim from a cold pond into the warmth from below. The hut is always equipped with a spotlight to offset any cold spells that may last for several days. Of course temperature dips below 64°F (18°C) are combated with

Only with the necessary knowledge and equipment can box turtles be kept in an outdoor pen in the summer.

a heating pad (see page 33) that is installed on the rear wall of the hiding place. This consists of a pile of straw or dry oak or beech leaves. To prevent heat buildup, darken the hiding place with a shade. Then it will stay appropriately warm even at night as early as May. Cooling below 54°F (12°C) must in any case be avoided (see page 59).

The Greenhouse: Comfortable

A greenhouse provides a turtle with a spacious, large terrarium with lots of room to roam. In addition, a hibernation box fits inside; it is installed flush with the floor. There are also add-on half-greenhouses that attach to the walls of a house and make it easier to provide heating, electricity, and water from the house. In addition, the wall of the house serves as a heat reservoir, as long as it is not insulated too efficiently.

Choice of Location The greenhouse should be exposed to morning sun. You can prevent an excess of midday sun with well-planned vegetation. In the summer, deciduous trees provide shade, but without leaves in the fall, winter, and spring, they allow all the sunlight through. The glass is usually double polycarbonate panes, which have adequate heat capture properties. An automatic, adjustable skylight opener (with thermostat and actuator) prevents heat buildup.

Setup A greenhouse for tortoises is set up on a simple ring-shaped foundation, but the setup for aquatic turtles is more demanding. The foundation does not go all the way around; it has a break of about 20 inches (50 cm) in the part that projects into the water so that the turtles can get in. Build the foundation before you put the pond liner into the pond. Then, in a single piece, put the liner

A cold frame is a secure hiding place. A rear wall made of stone stores up warmth, and the sliding door is closed at night for protection against predators.

over the pond, and the portion of the foundation that subsequently will be under water. An additional liner between the film and the concrete protects against damage. Once you have placed the greenhouse, the edge facing the pond is underwater by ⅜ inch to a little over 1 inch (1–3 cm). This keeps out unwanted draft.

Temperature Control In operating the greenhouse, remember that you must measure the temperature 2 to 4 inches (5–10 cm) above the ground level. It may still be cold there even though heat is accumulating in the upper part. You must provide heat at night in March because of the cold nights. A heater—electric or with a connection to the heating system in the house—keeps the space warm as needed. A low-hanging heat lamp completes the setup.

An Outdoor Pen on Terrace or Balcony

Sunny terraces and sturdy balconies that can support the weight of an installation also deserve consideration as locations for an outdoor pen. They contain the same elements as the indoor terrarium except for the lighting setup.

Main Structure This is made from wood, preferably of pressure-treated fence lath (from a lumber yard). Line the box with pond liner and use a knife to poke a few holes in the section of liner that covers the ground so that excess water can run off. Otherwise, the pen could become marshy.

Filling From bottom to top, this consists of a layer of expanded clay (from a gardening supplies store) 8 inches (20 cm) thick, a commonly available root barrier used as an underlay for lined ponds, and a layer of garden or forest soil. The latter should be high enough to keep the turtle from

Food plants such as *Egeria densa* and mouse-ear chickweed thrive in your pond; they are as tasty to your aquatic turtle as water snails.

climbing out. The expanded clay provides moisture storage and provides the soil with moisture through capillary action; the root barrier keeps a digging turtle from boring its way down to the expanded clay.

Roof This consists of two Plexiglas plates in a frame open to the eaves so that rain can run off readily (see illustration at right). Cut the sidewalls of the box at an angle 4 to 6 inches (10–15 cm) lower at the front than at the back. When the plate is in place, the result is a type of lean-to roof: rain runs off easily, and the sun shines in. Keep the panes in place with a rubber bungee cord so they don't blow open in a gust of wind.

Temperature Control When the sun is out, the pane is removed and stored behind the box; it is put back into place when the weather turns cold. This can also be accomplished with a thermal control of the type used for regulating simple ventilation flaps in small greenhouses. A couple of ¾ inch (2 cm) air holes drilled into the wood will provide ventilation even when the pane remains closed for several days. But when the pane is closed, regularly check the temperature. Shading the pane under which your animal has set up its resting place prevents additional heat accumulation and gives it a sense of security.

Draft There is a slight draft on balconies on upper floors even when there is no wind at ground level. A folding divider provides relief from this. A chicken-wire cover provides protection from crows.

Vegetation It's best to place potted plants next to the box so that the branches hang over it and provide shade as needed.

Even if you have no yard, a roomy pen on the balcony gives your turtle the possibility of outdoor accommodations. The water basin is made larger or smaller depending on need and turtle species. Land-dwelling pond turtles need a hiding place on land.

A Balcony Setup for Aquatic Turtles

Proceed essentially as with the planning for the tortoise pen. But instead of a swimming basin, install a mortar pan as a miniature pond, and adjust the dimensions, water depth, and structure according to the information for the indoor aquarium. Filter and empty the pond with a commercially available drain valve on the bottom. The bottom must be fitted with an appropriate hole. Use your aquarium filter.

Dangers on the **Balcony**

PREVENTING ESCAPES Close off all spaces between the floor and the balcony railing with boards so your pet does not take a fall if it gets out.

PROVIDE WARMTH The balcony pen must have a spotlight if you want to keep your pet in it until it gets ready for hibernation.

Healthy Turtles

Appropriate living conditions in a stimulating environment, adequate exercise, and healthy nutrition—these are the requirements that ensure your turtle's well-being. But health protection must not be given short shrift. Here is the best way to proceed.

Proper Feeding for Turtles

What Kind of Food? Tortoises are given fresh food and supplements of fresh hay. Aquatic turtles are fed according to the information in the Profiles section and on page 50 ff, with animal and possible plant foods in combinations and amounts that change on a daily basis. Young animals should be able to find animal food throughout the entire day. As they grow older, they are fed once or twice a day. Also, build in some days of fasting on which they get only a small snack of commercial food or a couple of water fleas. On the following day, give them a fish. This type of change corresponds to the quantities that are available in the wild.

When to Feed The timing depends on your turtle's active times. Animals that are active during the day get the majority (60–70%) of their food in the early morning and a smaller meal (30–40%) in the late afternoon. Species that are active at dusk get their food in the half-light of the morning and evening. Hay is given to tortoises as a supplement from spring through summer, and then as a nutritional base through the fall (see page 48).

How Much to Feed Here is how to determine the appropriate daily portion: Let your turtle fast for one day. On the following day, weigh the recommended food mix or measure it with a level teaspoonful. Feed the animal until its initial craving is satisfied and it eats noticeably more slowly or selectively. Now, determine how much the creature ate by weighing the leftovers and subtracting from the starting amount. From then on, feed only half the amount fed in the experiment. Check your pet's weight gain by weighing it regularly and keep a record.

Nutrition for Tortoises

In general, tortoises are "conservative eaters" and distrustful of anything new. Please note this with the important change of fodder and stick resolutely to your product choice. In the spring, everything should be fresh and high in nutrients; in the summer, the food should be dry and high in fiber, except for the fruits.

Staple Food—Economical and Good

Hay The best staple food for your tortoise is hay, and it should be provided fresh every day in the hay rack. It has a positive effect on digestion. Hay should smell like fresh black tea and must never smell musty. In addition to pesticide-free hay from farmers, you can also get mountain meadow hay for tortoises in small packages in pet shops.

Foliage For many years, I have had good experiences with cuttings of mulberry, willow, young birch, and hornbeam—but not from the side of the road. Grapevine leaves are also eaten with gusto as are hibiscus and forsythia. These are appropriate only if you are certain that they have not been sprayed.

The Best Standard Mix

The following menu will provide a healthy, fresh diet that is high in protein. It meets the need for protein, calcium, and phosphorus when mixed in the right proportions.

3½ ounces (100 g) of food mix contain the following:

> 3 ounces (80 g) romaine lettuce
> ½ ounce (12 g) apple
> 1/8 ounce (5 g) banana
> 1/32 ounce each of fruits, carrot, dandelion

Provide a Variety Replace the romaine lettuce with wild herbs such as goutweed, chickweed, and various types of plantain from your yard. Also white and red clover, dead-nettle, stinging nettle, hedge bindweed, and sweet pea are welcome meals. You can get tortoise-herb seeds (from pet shops) for planting in your garden. Make sure wild foods are not chemically sprayed.

Keeping Tabs European tortoises should never eat only fruits and leave the rest. The whole mixture must be consumed every day. If you determine that your pet eats the fruits enthusiastically but spurns the lettuce, then feed lettuce exclusively the following day—naturally, in fresh form. Watch your tortoise closely while it eats. This applies in particular to two tortoises that eat at the same dish. This is the only way to make sure that both animals are eating a balanced, healthy mix and getting their proper ration.

Scientifically Proven

Studies by C. Dennert (see Books, page 62) verify that an adult tortoise needs the following nutritional components:

> plant protein: 20% (25% for young animals)
> plant fats: less than 10%
> crude fiber: between 12 and 30%
> lime (calcium): 2%
> phosphorus: 1.2 %

An outdoor pen planted with various herbs provides tortoises with a variety of fresh appetizers.

Good hay is fed in increasing amounts from the start of summer to hibernation time. It has a positive effect on the intestinal flora.

Sprouts

These contain lots of vitamins, minerals, and fiber and are recommended for rounding out the fresh food every day. Retailers of seeds (health food stores, natural food shops) also have appropriate containers for sprouting and precise directions. Seeds are watered and raised in different ways, depending on what type they are.

My Tip Sprouted wheat 3 inches (10 cm) high is also very good for making crickets nutritionally more valuable before feeding them to aquatic turtles. Let crickets graze on sprouted wheat before feeding the crickets to your tortoise.

Nutritional Supplements

Lime Your tortoise's food should contain 1.5 to 2 times more calcium than phosphorus; this is ensured in the food mixtures mentioned previously. In addition, provide calcium in the form of a cuttlebone (from a pet shop), which your tortoise can nibble as desired. The need for calcium is particularly high among young animals and females in the egg formation phase.

Vitamins and Trace Elements These are probably not needed if your tortoise is fed with fresh (live) food, gets UV light, and lives outdoors in the summertime. If needed, these are administered only in consultation with a veterinarian.

Commercially Prepared Foods

Given the number of turtle species, commercially manufactured foods sometimes do not meet the requirements of your tortoise. When you buy food, make sure that the nutrients mentioned on page 48 are listed in amounts that are not significantly higher or lower. Before buying, check the commercial mixes to be sure the right information is contained on the packaging. Commercial food is no match for fresh food when used as a sole food source.

Nutrition for Aquatic Turtles

In contrast to most tortoises, the aquatic turtles mentioned in this handbook are fed with an assortment of foods. That is, they consume plants and small creatures. The latter—referred to in dietary science as "animal protein"—are found on the land in the form of insects and other small creatures such as crickets, grasshoppers, bugs and their larvae, spiders, woodlice, centipedes, earthworms, and snails. Crustaceans that young animals prefer are found in the water; these include water fleas, insects and their larvae (mosquito larvae, water

1 Insect larvae (*Zophobas* in this case) can be given as the sole offering on fasting days or occasionally as supplements to the staple diet (fish, crustaceans, snails).

2 Species that eat little or no plant food, such as this European Pond Turtle, leave your pond plants mostly undisturbed.

bugs), mollusks (mussels and snails), young whole fishes, and amphibians and their larvae (tadpoles).

A Varied Diet

Young aquatic turtles eat meat almost exclusively, as long as they live in the water. The Eastern Box Turtle gradually shifts over to a mixed diet with increasing age. As it grows older, the Striped Mud Turtle consumes about 75% meat and the rest as plants; this is also true of the Red-bellied Short-necked Turtle. European Pond Turtles also prefer about 90% fresh food in advanced age, and the Common Musk Turtle feeds exclusively on meat for its entire life.

Aspic Food—Long Lasting and Nutritionally Complete

For aquatic turtles, food in the form of aspic is unbeatable because of the variety of possible applications and ease of handling. The following "recipe" is chosen with consideration and contains everything required for your turtle's healthy nutrition. You can change the taste as needed with additives such as squid, shellfish, and fresh shrimp.

Basic Recipe For about 3 pounds (1.3 kg) you will need the following:
> 14 ounces (400 g) fresh water fish, whole
> 7 ounces (200 g) beef heart
> 7 ounces (200 g) squid, natural
> 10 ounces (300 g) shrimp or krill (in pellet form with 50% protein, from feed store)
> 2 chicken eggs with shells
> shells from two chicken eggs or a cuttlebone

› up to 7 ounces (200 g) greens—depending on your animal's dietary needs—in the form of young stinging nettle leaves, arugula, clover, chickweed, carrots, apples, whole-grain cooked rice, or hominy.

Preparation All the ingredients are thoroughly washed, and the meat—separated from the rest of the ingredients—is pureed with water in a high-speed blender to a mash with the consistency of honey. Mix everything well and heat to 176°F (80°C). While stirring constantly, let the entire mixture cool down to about 122°F (50°C), and then, according to instructions, add food gelatin and a vitamin and mineral mix from the veterinarian. Look for good-quality gelatin; this is the only kind that does not subsequently degrade in warm water. Let the mass congeal on a baking pan. Then you can divide it into daily portions and deep-freeze it for 6 months in plastic bags. On nutritional grounds, the 6-month storage should not be exceeded, in order to avoid decomposition. For omnivores and primarily vegetarians, the aspic should be given only as a supplement while feeding fresh plant material.

Commercially Manufactured Food

This food is formulated generally and may not always meet the dietary guidelines in this handbook. For omnivores and pure carnivores, the food consists of extrudates with a 40–50% protein content and 4–5% fat content. If you don't see information about the calcium-phosphorus proportion (about 2:1), use it only as "activity food" in the smallest amounts for fasting days, and never as a sole source of food for raising young animals or for adults.

Raising or Buying **Food Animals**

TIPS FROM
TURTLE EXPERT
Dr. Hartmut Wilke

BREEDING OR CATCHING You can breed water fleas, earthworms, and crickets in containers at home. You can find complete instructions in *My Turtle* (see Books, page 62). If you want to catch the creatures yourself, be sure to comply with fish and game and environmental regulations.

BREEDING WATER SNAILS Commercially available snails (from pet shops) are easy to breed in an aquarium with a capacity of 10 to 16 gallons (40–60 l). Set up the aquarium in a well-lighted place without heat or lighting and fill it three-quarters full with water. Plant it full of *Egeria densa* and "fertilize" it with a pinch of fish food. Start with six to twelve snails of a single species. Depending on the family, they will eat the algae and the suspended matter on the surface of the water and on the bottom. Feed them additionally with flake food.

LIVE FOOD (FROM A PET SHOP) A large variety of live food is available all year. The selection includes water fleas, crickets, enchitraeids, and tubifex (rinse thoroughly).

Necessary Care Measures

As a responsible turtle owner, you should develop a feel through observation for how your pet shows that it is feeling well or signaling an emergency. That way, you can intervene in a timely

A healthy turtle will always look at you attentively when you approach the terrarium.

fashion to ensure the animal's health and vitality. Consistent care is the best way to ensure your pet's good health.

Terrarium Care

› Remove droppings and leftover food every day, and scrub out the water bowl with hot water, a brush, and unscented detergent.
› Every two weeks, scoop out the damp dirt between the water basin and the land portion with a soup spoon and replace it with fresh soil, for it can be a breeding ground for intestinal parasites.

Aquarium Care

› Remove droppings and leftover food from the filter or from the floor of the aquarium every day. Clean these places by siphoning with a hose. For hygienic reasons, do not suck with your mouth, but rather fill the hose by submerging it in the aquarium water. Stop the end of the hose with your thumb and open it only when the other end in your hand is lower than the water level in the tank.
› Change the water every two to three days if you are caring for one young animal in only 3 to 6 gallons (10–20 l) of water.
› Every one to three weeks (depending on the condition of the water), change a third of the water and rinse out the filter with cold, clear water. That way you do not harm the useful microbes that live on it and condition the water.
› Once a month, let the water out of the aquarium and remove the waste buildup from the corners. Clean the roots and panes of glass with a sponge. In the meantime, your turtle should stay in its quarantine container. Before putting the turtle back in, the water is brought up to the appropriate temperature.

Checking the Turtle

By way of further preventive measures, you should observe and regularly check your pet, its behavior, and its development.

› Every day during the activity phase, check if the behavior and appetite are normal.

› Once a week, pick up the animal and inspect the plastron, the deep skin folds, and the anal region for physical integrity and cleanliness. Also check the eyes, mouth, and breathing sounds.

› Once a month, weigh the turtle and write down the results.

› In August of every year, have the veterinarian check a stool sample and the turtle's health.

A Health Check

Even as a beginner, you can determine your turtle's health by checking both its body and its behavior—preferably at point of purchase. The following characteristics indicate a healthy turtle.

› The weight feels like you are holding a stone of similar size in your hand.

› Young turtles flail with front and hind legs when they are picked up; adults pull into their shell (defensive behavior).

› The eyes are clear, with no mucous formation, and neither sunken nor swollen.

› The eardrum (behind the eyes) is smooth and does not bulge outward.

› The nose is dry and free of both discharge and little bubbles. Breathing is silent.

› The inside of the mouth is pink—not dark red—and free of pasty or other coatings.

› The limbs are firm and not noticeably swollen or thin.

› The anus displays no inflammation or swelling and is clean.

1 BASKING Outstretched legs and lowered head are common while basking; however, if this is an ongoing condition, they are a sign of serious weakness.

2 PEELING If individual scutes or sections of skin come loose, there is no reason for concern. Sometimes this is entirely normal with many aquatic turtles.

3 CALCIUM REQUIREMENT Young turtles and pregnant females have a high need for calcium; a cuttlebone from a pet shop will satisfy this need.

Unusual Behaviors

The turtle spends a lot of time lying under the spotlight and appears languid. In addition to an illness, the reason may be a setup that is too cold. Or a sexually mature female could be encouraging egg development by means of the warmth. In the first case, determine your pet's preferred temperature range. In the second case, leave the female in peace but continue to observe her.

The turtle continually changes its preferred whereabouts. If you suddenly find your aquatic turtle on land, and it is not looking for a place to bask or to lay eggs, perhaps the water has become too warm or too cold. A tortoise reacts to excessively warm or cold terrariums by digging shallowly and apathetically into the coolest corner. Solution: check the temperature every day and, if necessary, restore the water temperature to the temperature ranges specified in the Profile.

A healthy throat area is pink and smooth like this. It must be free of coatings and foamy bubbles.

The turtle walks or swims around restlessly. There may be many reasons for this.
› Social stress, if several creatures live in the same setup. Separate the creatures.
› Sexually mature females react in this way to egg binding (see next section).
› The temperature is not right. Check the thermometer daily and provide the temperature ranges specified in the Profiles.
› Disturbances such as draft, vibrations from machines or stereos, and strong odors such as fireplace or tobacco smoke can lead to this behavior. Take corrective action.

Possible Symptoms of Illness

Swollen Eyelids The eyes are shut and swollen. This could also be caused by draft, foreign object, injury, or a vitamin A deficiency; with aquatic turtles, water contaminated with bacteria could also be the cause. Visit the veterinarian.

Increased Restlessness A sexually mature female walks around restlessly all day long and behaves more like a tortoise by staying on land. She may dig holes but is not able to lay the eggs. In extreme conditions the heels of the hind legs are rubbed sore. Causes: The animal is suffering from egg binding. Remedy: Check if the depth of the egg-laying location is at least 1.5 times the length of the shell. If it is, visit the veterinarian immediately.

Shortness of Breath The turtle stretches its neck far out, opens its mouth, and makes peeping, moaning, or snoring noises. It keeps lowering its head in fatigue. Causes: Serious illnesses. Remedy: You must avoid warming the turtle. Immediately bring it to the veterinarian, where it will have to be x-rayed.

Creating an Appropriate Environment

As long as the terrarium climate, the nutrition, the hygiene conditions, and the necessary space are provided, the turtle probably will develop to be healthy and live to an old age.

Appropriate

- (+) If there is no outdoor pen available to the tortoise, a winter garden set up as a terrarium with a run of 6 to 12 square feet (2–4 m²) will be a good substitute.

- (+) A hiding place made of bricks inside the greenhouse will store up warmth for cold nights. It delays the undesirable temperature fall.

- (+) For healthy hibernation, tortoises are given only about 50% of the usual amount of fresh food starting in September. From October on, they receive no further fruit, but only hay.

- (+) An outdoor pen needs the same care as an aquarium or a terrarium, especially with respect to hygiene.

Questionable

- (−) Tortoises should never spend their whole life in a terrarium—that is "incarceration."

- (−) In the spring, do not let the turtle in the outdoor pen cool down below 54°F (12°C). That is a drain on the energy stores and is harmful to health.

- (−) Tortoises should not be fed year round only with nutrient-poor types of lettuce and/or dry food; otherwise, there is a danger of nutritional deficiency.

- (−) Don't believe that your turtle can fend for itself outdoors without your care. It is living in an unfamiliar climate.

The Turtle in Hibernation

As early as August of every year, you should take a stool sample according to the veterinarian's instructions, and if necessary treat your turtle for worms under the veterinarian's guidance. That way there is enough time to treat and cure any illnesses before hibernation.

Prelude to Hibernation

Your healthy, wormed turtle may still be walking or swimming around in the **indoor terrarium** in October or November, but without eating anymore. Now lower the air and/or water temperature in the installation in three or four steps of 4–6°F (2–3°C) over three to five days each, for a total of 18–20°F (10–12°C). After about two weeks, the ambient temperature should be around 59–63°F (15–17°C). At this time most species will have no appetite, empty their intestine, dig into a dark corner, and provide a clear signal that they now wish to begin hibernation.

In a greenhouse—because of the temperature decrease and the shortening of the days—the turtle will voluntarily go into its hibernation box without any assistance from you. As soon as it moves into its winter quarters, turn off the heat and the lamps.

The Right Hibernation Temperature

Whether on land or in water, your turtle generally hibernates at 39–43°F (4–6°C). But since the wintertime temperatures in the wild are not the same every year, in my experience your pet can deal with temperature increases up to 50–54°F (10–12°C) without a problem (without becoming active). In this context I refer to the very useful scientific research by Pawlowski (see Scientific Articles, page 62). Note, however, the exceptions for species for which the hibernation temperature may be higher in the wild (see Profiles, page 20 ff.).

Wintertime Checks and Controls

Tortoises Before hibernation, weigh your animal and write down the weight. Because of the stable climate in the hibernation box, this needs to be checked only every three weeks. Does the hygrometer still show humidity of 70–90% in the place where the tortoise has dug in?

In our latitudes, tortoises should not hibernate in the backyard pond. Many die in it.

How does the installation smell? Nothing should have mold, smell musty, or be wet. You absolutely must replace any wet or moldy soil or leaves. If things are too dry for the tortoise, carefully moisten the layer of expanded clay without dribbling on the animal's lair. Weigh your tortoise every three weeks and write down the weight.

Aquatic Turtles Check your animal and the winter quarters once a week. If the water is clear it does not need to be changed. Before a water change (in case of cloudiness), if necessary cool down the fresh water to the required winter temperature. Change the oak leaves and clean the basin with a sponge and clear water.

1 BATH TIME Generally it is not necessary to bathe a tortoise before hibernation. In proper living conditions that are not too dry, the tortoise will spontaneously empty its intestine. If it does not do this "voluntarily" and yet shows all signs of hibernation (see page at left), bathe it in 75°F (24°C) water. This will stimulate intestinal activity and encourage complete evacuation.

2 AUTUMN Initially the tortoise declines to take in any food. A few days later its activity decreases when it finds a dark, damp, deep hiding place in the terrarium where it intends to hibernate. It will stay there until you place your pet into its winter quarters at a lower temperature.

3 DISAPPEARANCE This is the aquatic turtle's goal in the fall. In the wild, it digs into the mud or under roots on the shore. Instead of this, you can provide free-floating oak leaves. Their tannin inhibits germs, but you still need to change the water immediately if it becomes cloudy. Darken the winter quarters with a cover or a sheet of plastic.

Disturbances During Hibernation

When a turtle changes position infrequently or remains immobile, it is a clear sign that hibernation is approaching. But if your tortoise or aquatic turtle shows ongoing restlessness, the hibernation has been disturbed. In this case, check if your animal has lost more than 10% of its body weight. If so, interrupt the hibernation, slowly warm up your pet (see right), and take it to the veterinarian. Thereafter, the tortoise must be properly cared for according to the veterinarian 's recommendations and under normal conditions in the terrarium or aquarium.

An Orderly Emergence from Hibernation

A tortoise ends its winter rest between March and April and spends a day sitting on the leaves. Now put it into the terrarium and keep it at 60–64°F (16–18°C) for two to three days, and then another two days at 64–68°C (18–20°C). Thereafter it may bathe in a solution of table salt in warm water at 72° (22°C) (⅓ ounce/9 g of salt to just over 1 quart of water/1 l). The tortoise can drink and compensate for fluid loss. Then bring the terrarium up to the right temperature. Offer the tortoise fresh food every day; after a week it will eat.

In a roomy outdoor pen like this one, a turtle can be outdoors and search for food as early as warm March days. If it gets colder, the greenhouse provides adequate space for its activities.

An **aquatic turtle** signals the end of hibernation through increased activity. Bring the hibernation box including the turtle into a well-lighted space with no heat, where it can slowly warm up to 60–64°F (16–18°C) over two days. Also remove the cover. Then place your animal into the aquarium or aquaterrarium at the same temperature. Now increase the temperature of the air and water by 4°F (2°C) increments over the course of two days until the temperature appropriate for the species are reached. The turtle will start eating again after about a week.

For hibernation in the refrigerator, take out the container with the turtle at the given time and place it for two days in an unheated room at 54–59°F (12–15°C). That way the temperature can slowly equalize, and the turtle can become acclimatized. Then place your pet into the unheated terrarium at 64°F (18°C) for another two days. Wait until the animal begins to walk around. Then, when it is really active and awake, turn on the heat and the lights.

Coming Out of Hibernation in a Greenhouse

The turtle will wake up as early as February or March because of the heating power of the higher sun. This is advantageous for reproduction, which starts earlier, so that the young reach a suitable size before their first hibernation. Now turn on the heat and lighting as recommended for the terrarium. You can even put your turtle right into the terrarium or aquarium temporarily until the nights in the greenhouse no longer fall below 60–64°F (16–18°C). Thereafter avoid temperature drops below 54°F (12°C) outdoors. That would weaken the immune system and become life threatening. Otherwise proceed as described above for tortoises and aquatic turtles.

Information About **Hibernation**

TIPS FROM
TURTLE EXPERT
Dr. Hartmut Wilke

EXTENDING HIBERNATION Is your pet hibernating in a greenhouse, and do you want to wait until you can pick fresh dandelions for food? Then put off your pet's awakening for a while by ventilating the greenhouse well. Protect the hibernation pit from the day's warmth with a Styrofoam sheet so it cannot reach your turtle.

NO OUTDOOR HIBERNATION You may have heard recommendations saying that it is possible in our latitudes for tortoises to hibernate in the yard, and for aquatic turtles to hibernate in a pond. I advise strongly against this. Most areas in our latitudes are absolutely inappropriate for this, for the spring is too variable and cold for too long. For most turtles this manner of hibernation is certain death.

PATIENCE WITH EMERGENCE FROM HIBERNATION Warming up too quickly to the terrarium temperature that I have provided in this book goes contrary to the conditions in nature, and in some cases it can prove fatal to the turtle.

Organizations

There are many organizations for turtle and tortoise enthusiasts. The easiest way to locate them is to search online; a number of Internet sites are mentioned here.

Turtles on the Internet

› www.nytts.org
The New York Turtle and Tortoise Society.
› www.sdturtle.org
The San Diego Turtle and Tortoise Society.
› www.matts-turtles.org
The Mid-Atlantic Turtle and Tortoise Society.
› www.turtleforum.com
A forum for turtle care and support.
› www.reptilechannel.com
The website for reptile lovers, with a turtles and tortoises section.
› www.boxturtlesite.info
The place to learn about Box Turtles.
› www.tortoise.org
The California Turtle and Tortoise Club.
› www.geocities.com/heartland/village/76666/
The Chicago Turtle Club—for help in maintaining the well-being, safety, and environment of turtles and tortoises.

Books

› Bartlett, R. D., and Patricia Bartlett. *Aquatic Turtles: Sliders, Cooters, Painted, and Map Turtles.* Hauppauge, NY: Barron's Educational Series, 2003.
› ___. *Box Turtles: Facts and Advice on Care and Breeding.* Hauppauge, NY: Barron's Educational Series, 2001.
› ___. *Turtles and Tortoises—A Complete Pet Owner's Manual.* Hauppauge, NY: Barron's Educational Series, 2006.
› Cook, Tess. *Box Turtles—Complete Herp Care.* Neptune City, NJ: TFH Publications, 2004.
› Cursen, Sarah. *Those Terrific Turtles.* Sarasota, FL: Pineapple Press, 2006.
› Flank, Lenny, Jr. *The Turtle: An Owner's Guide to a Happy, Healthy Pet.* Kindle Book, 1997.
› Kirkpatrick, David. *Aquatic Turtles—Complete Herp Care.* Neptune City, NJ: TFH Publications, 2006.
› Palika, Liz. *Turtles and Tortoises for Dummies.* New York, NY: Hungry Minds, 2001.
› Patterson, Jordan. *The Guide to Owning a Box Turtle,* Neptune City, NJ: TFH Publishing, 2005.
› Wilke, Hartmut. *Turtles—A Complete Pet Owner's Manual.* Hauppauge, NY: Barron's Educational Series, 2006.

Magazines

› *Herp Digest* (free Internet magazine), www.herpdigest.org.

Scientific Articles

› For a long list of articles by D. Kirkpatrick, visit www.unc.edu/~dtkirkpa/stuff/biblio.html.
› Pawlowski, Sascha. 2004. "Successful indoor hibernation of several freshwater turtle species at temperatures of 12–15° C." *Radiata* (English Edition). 13(2): 3–9 [spawlows@ix.urz.uni-heidelberg.de].

Important **Notice**

› Electrical devices The electrical devices for terrarium care described in this book must be properly grounded. Be aware of the dangers of dealing with electronic devices and wires, especially in conjunction with water. Obtaining an electronic surge protector is recommended.
› Hygiene Be sure to pay attention to your personal hygiene and wash your hands after contact with the animals.

English Translation © Copyright 2010 by Barron's Educational Series, Inc.
© Copyright 2009 by Gräfe und Unzer Verlag GmbH, Munich, Germany

The title of the German book is *Schildkröten*
English translation by Eric Bye

All inquiries should be addressed to:
Barron's Educational Series, Inc.
250 Wireless Boulevard
Hauppauge, NY 11788
www.barronseduc.com

ISBN-13: 978-0-7641-4498-1
ISBN-10: 0-7641-4498-7

Library of Congress Catalog Card No.: 2010004327

Library of Congress Cataloging-in-Publication Data
Wilke, Hartmut, 1943-
    [Schildkr?ten. English]
    Turtles: everything about selection, care, nutrition, and behavior/ Hartmut Wilke.
        p. cm.
    Includes bibliographical references and index.
    ISBN-13: 978-0-7641-4498-1 (alk. paper)
    ISBN-10: 0-7641-4498-7 (alk. paper)
1. Turtles as pets. I. Title.
SF459.T8W5413 2010
639.3'92—dc22   2010004327

PRINTED IN CHINA
9 8 7 6 5 4 3

The Author

Dr. Hartmut Wilke is a biologist and has accumulated a professional lifetime of practical experience as the director of the Exotarium at the Frankfurt Zoo and the director of the Darmstadt Zoo (both in Germany). He has always provided advice to inquiring turtle hobbyists. This manual benefits greatly from this.

The Photographer

Christine Steimer works as a freelance photographer and specializes in pet photography. She works for international book publishers, professional journals, and advertising agencies. All photos in this book are by Christine Steimer, except for **Getty-images**: 6, 7-1; **Juniors:** 7-2.

Translator

Eric Bye, M.A., C.T. is a freelance translator of German, French, and Spanish who lives and works in Vermont. He has translated many pet books for Barron's.

SOS—What to Do?

Escaped

PROBLEM Your tortoise has disappeared from the outdoor pen. **THIS MAY HELP** Look for sunny spots in the early morning hours. If your tortoise has left the yard, it may try to get back in. So look along the outside of the fence.

Peeling

PROBLEM Large pieces or sections of my aquatic turtle's scales are coming loose. **THIS MAY HELP** With many species of aquatic turtle this condition is normal. This is also how they get rid of a possible algae growth, which is harmless. But if you detect offensive smells or bleeding, the turtle needs to see the veterinarian.

Getting Ready for Hibernation

PROBLEM It is fall, and the turtle has no more appetite and digs in. **THIS MAY HELP** It is telling you that it wants to go into hibernation. Stop feeding it, make sure it empties its intestine, and turn off both heat and light. Then let it hibernate.

Major Restlessness

PROBLEM Your turtle walks around restlessly, digs in the soil with its front feet, and continually uses its nose to check the texture. It digs deep holes with its hind legs. **THIS MAY HELP** Presumably this involves a female experiencing egg binding. Provide your animal with a thoroughly damp, warm ground. If the turtle does not lay its eggs within 12 hours in the newly configured place, you should promptly take it to the veterinarian.

Foam on the Eye

PROBLEM The corners of the eye are filled with foam from one day to the next. The phenomenon may last for days or weeks. **THIS MAY HELP** The Harderian glands located under the nictating membrane, which produce a protective film for the eyes, may be working overtime. It is not yet clear if this occurs because of stress, the effect of excessively dry air, or mechanical reasons during food intake. Check the points mentioned and keep a record.